First Generation Singular: Reactions to Living in Post-Holocaust Germany

First Generation Singular: Reactions to Living in Post-Holocaust Germany

in Poetry and Prose

SHIRLEE SKY HOFFMAN

Front cover design and art: Susan Bruck

The transliteration of the Hebrew word on the cover is *zachor;* it means "remember."

ISBN: 1533660654
ISBN 13: 9781533660657
Library of Congress Control Number: 2016909404
CreateSpace Independent Publishing Platform
North Charleston, South Carolina

Contents

Preface

I STILL HAVE the book on the bottom shelf of the bookcase in our living room, on the right hand side as you face the fireplace: *The Scourge of the Swastika: A Short History of Nazi War Crimes*, by Lord Russell of Liverpool. From this book, which I discovered in the basement of my childhood home in Toronto, Canada, I learned the horrific scope of the Holocaust. Lord Russell's book, published in 1954, was, however, not my first consciousness of the Holocaust. I don't remember exactly what was.

Candidates for my initiation include, when I was almost seven, reading *The Diary of Anne Frank* during our family's summer vacation at Wapaska Lodge in Muskoka, the popular vacation area north of Toronto. At Wapaska Lodge, too, one of the kitchen staff had a number tattoo on her forearm that adults quietly referenced as an explanation when excusing her volatile temper. Or perhaps my parents talked about the devastation, but I can't remember anything specific. I don't remember them referring to relatives left behind in Russia as being known victims of the Holocaust.

I'm guessing that Heinz Warschauer, the director of education at our synagogue, Holy Blossom Temple, was a significant factor in my dawning awareness. I'm sure I had been told early on that he, so notable because of his heavy German accent, was a survivor (whatever that was) who had been in Buchenwald (whatever that was). Heinz had indeed been incarcerated in Buchenwald. He had been—I don't know how—able to get out to England before the outbreak of World War II. From there, he and other German Jews, mistakenly identified as enemy aliens and not Jewish refugees, had been sent on to confinement in Canada. By 1943, through the efforts of the Canadian Jewish community and a high-ranking diplomat sent by the British, they had all finally been released.

Looking back, it seems to me that the Holocaust has always been as much a part of my sense of who I am as the Yiddish name, *Sora Liba Channah*, my mother made sure I knew was mine. It was, therefore, little surprise that the Holocaust and my two experiences of living in Germany, in 1970–71 and 1976–77, amalgamated together to generate a group of poems. Since my early teen years, poetry has been my preferred medium for capturing what is currently bubbling up out of the impenetrable soup of my subconscious.

For two or three days a week during several months in early 1988, responding to an unequivocal and unavoidable compulsion, I sat in front of a computer screen, which at that time displayed amber letters against a black background, and watched the poems that named themselves *First Generation Singular* form. I didn't seem to have much choice. As each poem presented itself, the words lined up and plopped themselves in place with relatively little revision. Relentlessly. Then one day the words stopped. The flow clotted and stanched itself. After that, on the subject of my experiences in Germany and the reflections on the Holocaust they engendered, there was no more until 1993, when a trip that included Weimar occasioned one final poem.

Soon after that trip I assembled a document containing the originals of the poems you will be reading here; my mother's fictionalized writings, mostly about her early childhood in Russia;

and my father's autobiography about his youth as an immigrant to Canada, all strung together with explanatory commentary. I called the totality the *Sky Family Festschrift* and distributed it, in a very limited, self-produced print edition, to my extended family and close friends. The end—or so I thought.

Fast forward to March 2015 when, because my husband wanted to hear the music, I found myself sitting in the audience at the Lyric Opera of Chicago watching a performance of Mieczysław Weinberg's *The Passenger.* The opera tells the story of a female SS overseer in Auschwitz who, while she is travelling with her German-diplomat husband on a ship bound for Brazil, comes face to face with one of her former prisoners. The scenery portrayed the deck of an ocean liner suspended over a bare barrack room in the death camp.

I lasted through the first act, unable to suspend disbelief adequately in the face of robust chorus members or the travesty of only one of the characters being identified as Jewish. While I sat squirming in my seat, my mind fastened on the poems I had written over two decades before. It was time to revisit the poems, rework them, and consider trying to make them available to a wider audience. With the passing of years and of the Holocaust survivors, the baton of collective memory was mine to grasp, to carry forward. It was now my responsibility to use what I have, my poems, and their exploration of the broader paradoxes and complexities of my encounter with post-Holocaust Germany, to become an active participant in striving to ensure *Never Again* for the Jewish people and—hope against hope—for all humanity.

What you are reading is the result of that decision. I have edited and revised the poems and the accompanying commentary from their *Sky Family Festschrift* origins, often considerably. Their essence, though, and their dedication to the memory of the six million Jews that Nazi Germany persecuted from 1933 to 1945 and slaughtered with inconceivably successful single-mindedness from 1939 to 1945, remains the same.

Finally, a note about the glossary: As you read *First Generation Singular: Reactions to Living in Post-Holocaust Germany,* you will come across words and phrases in German, Yiddish, Hebrew, and even Aramaic. You will also find probably unfamiliar English phrases such as "white steak." In many cases I have included translations or synonyms as an integral part of the text. When I haven't, I direct you to the glossary where I hope I have provided adequate explanations. Should I have failed, I apologize, and refer you to the Internet where I am confident you will find what you seek.

Poetry and Prose

First Generation Singular

Why "First Generation Singular"

I HAVE ENTITLED this collection of poetry and prose *First Generation Singular* to signal the double perspective from which it was written: my own and my generation's.

My own status as a first-generation Canadian was not immediately obvious. My parents both spoke unaccented English, except for my father's failure to master the "th" sound in the middle of words, something which quite humorously showed up frequently because my childhood best friend's name was Dorothy. Nonetheless, since both my parents had been born in Russia—my father in Odessa and my mother in Dubrowo in the Russian Pale of Settlement—I was, invisibly, a first-generation Canadian. Only when I began writing these poems did it strike me that I was "first generation" in another previously unnoticed way. Born in October 1945, I was part of the first cohort of Jews who began life in the years immediately after the official end of World War II and, for this purpose, the Holocaust, on May 8, 1945, when Nazi Germany officially surrendered on all fronts.

First Generation Singular

Conceived before the end of the duration,
queued up to be one of the first generation,
like them, survivors' children,
I too was an affirmation,
a retort to death.

In 1943 and 1944,
within nine months, untimely dead,
my mother's mother, my mother's oldest brother.
Their deaths,
skimpy in comparison but still a devastation,
threw my mother for a loop
to the bottom.

Mother of two, she was considered old, then,
for conceiving more children.
Thirty-five, thirty-seven, thirty-nine—who knew?
The first day of Pesach as her birth date
gave no more clue than rumors
of the siblings' nudged-up ages
on her father's immigration papers.

Perhaps no longer able,
she took her doctor's advice,
his prescription for potential distraction,
to give it a try.

My birthing cries
broke death's hold on her spirit
and issued it entrée into mine,
a member of the first generation.

Viewed from this perspective,
my existence diminished both
my mother's and our people's
desolation.

Fraternizing with Past Enemies

How I Ended Up Living in Germany, Twice

"YOU WON'T FIND it boring," is what my future husband said to me at some point in our negotiation about becoming more closely involved with each other. That one short sentence is most likely the key to explaining how I ended up living twice in Germany, a country I hated for having produced the Nazis who destroyed one-third of my people.

The first time we headed off to Germany was in early July 1970, right after my husband, freshly graduated from law school, finished his two-week Army Reserve summer-camp obligation for the year. To his great delight, he had managed, through one of his professors, to be admitted to an exchange program that normally ran between an American university he had not attended and the *Institut für ausländisches und internationales Wirtschaftsrecht* at the Goethe University in Frankfurt am Main. The program included airfare for both of us, a reasonable monthly stipend, and a year's study at the university's law school for him.

Our year did not begin auspiciously. The flight to Frankfurt on the recently introduced Boeing 747 was aborted by an oil leak somewhere just short of the point of no return. We had to fly back to Kennedy Airport and stay another night with our Long Island relatives. My husband, fighting a flu bug, couldn't have cared less. He had no sympathy at all for my sensitivity to this obvious sign from above that I was not intended to reach the evil land of Germany alive. I was so thoroughly unnerved that before we again boarded the flight the next day, I took my first ever antianxiety pill.

Then there was my experience in the public toilets at the Frankfurt airport. I saw the plate of coins when I entered the ladies' washroom. I had been in Germany briefly during four months of European wanderings in 1968 after I'd dropped out of graduate school for the first time. I had a vague memory that I was supposed to leave some small payment. But there was no attendant to consult and, in my jet-lagged state, it may not have occurred to me to make change from the dish of coins, or perhaps I simply didn't have any German money yet. I used the facilities. As I started to wash my hands, a male janitor appeared, broom in hand, and seeing? assuming? I hadn't left anything, began yelling at me. My "for reading knowledge" German was not up to the challenge.

Frustrated, angered, embarrassed, bewildered, cursing wildly, I fled to give my husband a piece of my mind. I wanted to get out of this "Land of the Huns," a characterization I, a history major, knew to be not historically accurate. Right now! Instead we headed off to the factory in the nearby small town of Russelsheim, where we picked up our new car, an unattractively chartreuse-green Opel, and drove south to a Goethe Institute outside Munich. There, for a brief six weeks, we focused on transforming our previous disjointed and fragmentary encounters with German into the beginnings of fluency. Afterward we drove back north to begin what turned out to be a most enjoyable year in West Germany, the *Bundesrepublik Deutschland.*

The second time we made the journey to live in Germany, in 1976, it was because my husband wanted to spend a year at his international law firm's German office. With just a bit of timing adjustment to accommodate the birth of our first child, once again I found myself traveling to the "Land of the Huns." We flew to Milan, Italy, where we headed off to the nearby factory, picked up our new car, an unattractively moss-green Fiat, and drove over the Alps to the now very familiar, even comfortable, city of Frankfurt am Main, and, best of all, to our friends.

Our German Friends

OUR FIRST YEAR in Frankfurt was charmed. From among our contemporaries at the Institute, we quickly formed a small group of close friends. We got to know these Germans as individuals, people whom we came to appreciate and value deeply. They were our front line in experiencing post-Holocaust Germany.

We were all members of the borderless class known as "international student." Childless adults, we were without pressing time constraints or obligations beyond studying. My husband and I were also without a telephone, a modern convenience we'd taken for granted in North America that was not easily obtained in 1970 Frankfurt. Nonetheless, we readily managed to make arrangements to get together with our friends. We visited each other in various combinations, attending cultural events and partying together late into the night, passionately engrossed in long, involved theoretical discussions conducted in a convoluted German I often struggled to follow.

Through these friends we learned the nuances of German culture. For example, when should we use *Sie*, the formal form of "you," or *du*, the familiar form that was at that time still reserved for family, good friends, and children? When one of our new male acquaintances "dutzed" me—that is, addressed me as *du* immediately upon our being introduced—I found him rather insulting. I assumed, incorrectly it turned out, that he never would have "offered the *du*" to a German he had just met. He was, in fact, a committed egalitarian who addressed everyone as *du*.

On the other hand, what a strange feeling it was, the first time one of the couples invited us over to their apartment, to be called *Sie* and Herr and Frau Hoffman by people our own age. They served us peanuts and beer when we, unfamiliar with the clues, had anticipated supper. Similar miscues dogged us throughout both our stays. Either we stuffed ourselves only to be faced with a huge spread, or, ravenous and ready to eat, we were offered almost nothing. Our learning did not always go completely smoothly.

Through our friends, all of whom had studied English but who were willing to persist in speaking German with us, we learned the German language well beyond the Goethe Institute lessons. My husband and I marveled at how much easier it was to speak German with these people whom we knew so well. With them we felt comfortable enough just to spit it out, knowing they were more interested in what we were saying than how correctly it was being said. We even tried out cross-language jokes, believing them when they said we were being appropriately clever, laughing together on the few, but notable, occasions when my husband managed to know German opera lyrics they didn't.

Our close friends took it upon themselves that first year to show us Germany, both East and West. They brought us to the homes of their families and friends. At one time or another we took a trip with almost every one of them—to towns near Frankfurt, Stuttgart, Hamburg, the divided Berlin. People on the periphery of our close group also mediated our experiencing of post-Holocaust Germany. One of the women went out of her way to introduce us to her "Jewish friend" so that we would know there was still a Jewish presence in Germany. Hearing echoes of "some of my best friends are Jewish," we took her action in the amicable way it was intended.

We cherished our German friends during that first year when I started out more ready to damn it all than to enjoy our stay abroad, during our second year, and over the following years which saw almost annual visits on both sides of the Atlantic with them and their children. Even today, many years after we were last in Germany, we are still in touch with most of our friends. Our on-going relationships have created a vital, expanding buffer of positive memories that separates all of us from Germany's Nazi past. *First Generation Singular: Reactions to Living in Post-Holocaust Germany* in no way diminishes how precious those friendships remain to us today.

The Enigma

How to behave toward my enemy
in these new soothing moments of peace?
How to best honor ur-family
after the slaughter's final surcease?

Some say staunch, shunning separation.
Others preach healing, bridging outreach
to make strong the puny connection,
patch up the raw historical breach.

These questions I faced with the Germans:
yesterday's scourge that heinous portends;
today our good friends, simply humans
like us. With this my spirit contends.

Option 1: Staunch, Shunning Separation

Case 1: How Could You?
Sometime in the early 1950s,
when the first layer of scar tissue
had barely formed over the gouge in our people,
my best friend's older cousin,
the apple of the family's eye,
the *gutskeit,*
bought a s*chande,*
a Volkswagen Beetle.

Agonizing consternation and uproar ensued,
to no avail.
The People's Car—
that people's car—
remained.

Case 2: Telltale Marking
Later in the 1950s,
our first ever stereo record player,
hugely encased in heavy brown wood,
was carried by two Eaton's deliverymen
up our four concrete front steps
and carefully maneuvered
through our S-initialed aluminum screen door
to take up residence in our living room.

Briefly…
until my mother discovered the tattoo
"Made in West Germany"
needled into its stylus arm.
Back it went,
ASAP!

Case 3: Frankfurt Airport Willies
Persisting into the 1980s,
Frankfurt Airport Willies
was a common anxiety syndrome
among Jews.
When flying somewhere,
choose any other route—inconvenient, costly—
to avoid the brute of Frankfurt.

The JCC Board Institute,
vocally reluctant, fearful for their safety,
still chose the brute on their route.
How else to get to Poland?

Not yet sufficiently proven,
the purity of German intentions
when it comes to Jews.

When it came to Jews,
Germans intent on achieving purity,
on making Europe *judenrein*,
cleansed of Jews,
had not then, not so long ago then,
been focused on providing security.

Option 2: Healing, Bridging Outreach

For two years—twice one year—
I lived there, in Frankfurt,
where the Franks forded the river Main
for decade upon decade
many centuries ago
and where almost all the Jews vanished
during one half-decade
a while back.

Neither year was the Main choice mine.
Never had I said,
"Someday I must live in Germany.
Someday I must plunk myself down on the land
permeated with memories of my people's pain
and partake of its burgeoning harvest,
luxuriate in its present abundance."

We Jews had not ended well there
or in the lands the Nazis overwhelmed.
Why would I want to help them
do even a tiny bit better
with my dollars, my energy?

No, neither year was the Main choice mine.
But neither year was I willing to choose
away from my man.
Neither time was I willing to separate from him
and his choice.

"Why Germany?" I asked,
pleading with my question for a change of heart.
My pleas, directed at the wrong body part, failed.

I should have gone for his mind.
The Germanic mind—
Goethe, Schiller, Kant, Nietzsche,
Hegel, Heidegger, Strauss (Leo of course)—
had captured his.

I should have gone for his soul.
The Germanic soul—
Mozart, Beethoven, Schumann,
Schubert, Wagner, Strauss (Richard of course)—
had captured his.

I should have gone for his dick,
denied him all sexual privileges
until he reneged.

But then, not going along with his choice,
staying when he went,
would have had the same
unpleasant-for-both-concerned effect.

A rock and a hard place:
to stay near his hard places,
his two heads,
I chose the rock.

Perched on rock,
one can reach out
and build a bridge.

Linguistic Reverberations

Questions I Didn't Ask

Here, in the midst of Holocaust ruminations,
I must confess to questions
I didn't ask the implicated.

"Where were you?"
"What were you doing?"
"Why didn't you stop them?"

These questions I didn't ask
any of the older people in the streets where I walked.
I had the opportunity.
As I bopped along, my infant son in the backpack,
older people kindly stopped me,
tried to put his mittens back on
in vain pursuit of warm hands.

While they chuckled over him, tickled his cheek,
I did not ask them
whether they could tell he was Jewish,
whether they had stopped the Jewish children
being marched to the transports, toward the final consuming fire,
to put their mittens back on
in naïve foreshadowing of coming heat.

In the stores where I shopped,
I had the opportunity.
Every day older Germans waited on me.
"*Guten Tag*," they all said in greeting
when I walked *in den Laden*.

I, since they had started the conversation,
could easily have asked the questions,
slipped them in neatly
among my ordering phrases:

"*Hundert Gramm von dem, bitte.*"
"Where were you?"
"*Ja, ja, das reicht.*"
"What were you doing?"
"*Das wäre es, danke.*"
"Why didn't you stop them?"
"And by the way, whose store was this before the war?"

These questions I didn't ask
any of our German housekeepers, four in number,
hired over the years to speak German to our children
in vain pursuit of bilingualism.
Three of the housekeepers had been there,
old enough to have been doing adult things
and to have been able to act.

During the interviews I watched
for warmth, a loving nature, humor, compassion—
for everything but Nazi traces.
I asked the right child-rearing related questions
but not the others:
"Did you know any Jews in Germany?"
"Did you know what was happening to the Jews?"
"What did you feel as it was happening?"
"What do you think about what happened?"

"Where were you?"
"What were you doing?"
"Why didn't you stop them?"

Related questions neither have I ever asked, directly,
of our friends,
although there has been plenty of opportunity.

"Where were your parents?"
"What were they doing?"
"Why didn't they stop them?"

For one of our friends,
his father having finally resisted Hitler,
the answers were well known.
For the others,
any answer would be wrong.

The right answers
    "They were in the streets."
    "They were fighting against the Nazis."
    "They tried to stop them."
would be about people most probably dead,
long before they could have procreated.

It doesn't really matter now.
Any and all answers, right or wrong,
don't really matter now.
I know the end of the story.
Six million are dead and gone,
Forever.

Whatever the answers, they will not help me
understand, accept, reverse
the Forever.

Whatever the answers, they do not tell me how to
predict, determine, safeguard
the Future.

Maybe that is why there are so many questions
I still haven't asked.

Language Collaboration

So who won this one?
Them or me?
The Nazis or the Jew?

Yiddish,
my mother's mother tongue, my father's mother tongue,
the who knows how many others
related to me through gene soup's mother tongue,
Yiddish was lost to me.

Lost to me?
Positively denied to me by my parents,
speaking it when they didn't want me to understand.
No fear of leakage from behind.
They birthed me after all the grandparents had died
except my gossamer, pale, watery-eyed Zaide
who rarely spoke to me in any language.
My Bubbies would have.

Lost to me?
When I was trying to learn Hebrew, French, and Latin,
would that Yiddish had never been!

Instead Yiddish denied stood watch in my head,
chanting its false-logic cant,
protecting my porous brain cells against invasion:
    "Yiddish is forbidden to you.
    Yiddish is a foreign language.
    Foreign languages are forbidden to you."
Successfully too.

Mangled words and sentence structures
expired in piles at the feet of that Yiddish guard,
keeping me more or less foreign language *rein*,
although bare minimums of all three did seep in,
vastly reduced in strength—
grades of C-plus or B-minus strength, to be precise.

Lost to me
until I was dragged off to West Germany,
where I deked out the Yiddish guard,
punctured its defenses, breached the wall,
slayed it dead.

"Eureka! It is okay to learn a foreign language,"
I rejoiced as I cut off its head,
letting the loathsome German
come soaking in and oozing out
with heady fluency if not always perfection.

German, the verbal bayonets of the Nazis,
who eradicated six million of my people—
that cannot be said enough—
I learned their precision guttural, their mother tongue.
I slayed my Yiddish guard
in order to admit their venomous spikes.

So far,
looks like the German-speaking Nazis
won.

But wait, but, yet, what do I find?
Yiddish, my rightful mother tongue,
so long and so regrettably lost to me,
has become suddenly accessible, unexpectedly mine.

Without much effort,
    a little cock of the mind here,
    a little twist of a vowel there,
    a little "that must be a Hebrew or Slavic word" everywhere,
and my Yiddish guard, rising from the dead,
reset its head to sing a new-logic song:
    "German has been admitted by you.
    Yiddish is a foreign language very much like German.
    Yiddish is redeemed for you."
as it ushered the lost-to-me words of my mother tongue
into the spongy brain berths where they belong.

I didn't learn German to retrieve Yiddish.
The power of my new possession hadn't occurred to me
until the Yiddish in the movie *Hester Street* was
Eureka! without subtitles, sort of almost clear;
or until I could decipher the Hebrew letter *Arbetering* sign
on the cemetery gate. This was the place I was seeking.
My uncle, grandmother, and grandfather were buried here.

So who won this one?
The Jew.
By learning German I acquired Yiddish—almost free.
I declare this language collaboration a solid sweep for me!

Variations on a Beetle Theme

1.
Volkswagen.
The People's Car.
Still here, that Nazi star.

2.
She was a true friend
who, as late as 1964, asked
if I would mind riding
in her Beetle.
Ironically, specifically noted,
this car's heater wasn't strong enough
to warm, let alone cremate,
our bodies.

3.
Let's say John, Paul, George, and Ringo knew
what "Beetle" means
to many a Jew.
Might they instead
have chosen "Fleas"?
(But where to?)

4.
When breathing German air
every day in every way,
can you really care
if the car you rent
is a Beetle?

5.
"Slug bug yellow, slug bug blue,"
the carpool kids sang loud and true
whenever a Beetle came into view;
innocent players, too young to rue.

Number Games for the
Treasured People

Harvesting the Worst

"One of the basic principles of Jewish logic is that things
could always be worse."
—*The Big Book of Jewish Humor*

This time
things were
worse.

Six million,
one-third worldwide,
qualifies unequivocally as
worse.

Those times, too,
when Assyria dispersed the Northern Kingdom of Israel,
when Babylonia exiled the top slices of Judea,
when Rome pulverized Jerusalem and carried off the Temple
treasures,
things may conceivably have been
worse.

But how can we reliably know?
Those times happened so long ago,
before books and radio and film and video,
file cabinets full of documents,
or digital images at the click of a mouse,
all crystallizing our comprehension into inescapably concrete
worse.

This time, this last time,
things do appear to have been
worse.

And still, principles exploded, logic pulverized,
we Jews remain on course,
incurably addicted to our people,
searching among the ruins
for phoenix feathers.

Gluttons for life,
we replenish ourselves with Israel
as our tongues, *kvelling* over our ancestral land's virtues,
twist and turn with desperate agility
to avoid the raw hole of
worst
from which it emerged.

Malthus, What Do You Think?

How many of us could there have been,
we Jews,
if so many of us
had not been massacred?

If there had not been the Assyrians, Babylonians,
Greeks, Romans, Crusaders, Cossacks,
Nazis,
unter anderem (among others, as the Germans say),
would more of us have assimilated out?
Would more of us have somehow been left in?
Would our numbers have remained a constant?

Or, fortuitously unchecked by famine and disease,
would we have multiplied exponentially,
blanketed the world,
not only millions but billions of us,
officially turning all the little piggies into "white steak"
and creating an enormous market
for Shabbat, Havdalah, Channukah, and Yahrtzeit candles?

Taking a Broader Perspective

Hairsplitting?

What: Not Just Us
What's the problem?
The fuss, the muss, the fervor?

We weren't the only ones before.
We haven't remained the only ones since,
the only ones to be singled out
for being wiped out:
Stalin's millions, Mao's millions, Cambodians, Tutsis,
to mention just a recent few.
Whole chunks gone,
their blood, flesh, and bones mulch for their killers' crops.

How is our demise any different?

Why: Motives
Assiduously,
sparing no expense to the management,
they sought us out, to the very last one,
hidden under a floor or behind a wall.

Not for our ideas,
not for our land,
not for our power.

They killed us because
of our genes,
of our birth,
of our breath.
Nothing we could have said
would have stopped them.

Where: Centralized Processing
I would prefer,
kind Nazi sir,
if you would slay me where I live
as before, in days of yore,
your ancestors did their victims.

Don't
round me up, herd me together,
line me up, count me out,
march me to the forests,
or cram me tight into railroad freight cars
for the "final action."

If murder me you must
please do the deed where my neighbors can see.
In that there is some dignity, some humanity,
perforce some life-saving inefficiency.

How: Modern Science at Your Service
Any way in a pinch,
but the preferred, expedited method,
thanks to Nazi ingenuity, was a unique technique:
Zyklon B or some other poison gas,
into an airtight container,
finishing up with a hot oven
where bodies burnt to ash.

How Many Would Have Been Enough?

We anguish over six million,
but what if only five or four or three or two million,
or—what if only, if only—
what if almost none?

What if
the Nazi scissors had only snagged
not slashed our cloth?
Snip of warp, clip of weft,
familiar actions always in our history.

How many would have been enough,
quantity turned quality different enough,
to require a separate day for their memory,
a *Yom HaShoah*
instead of merely being folded into *Tisha B'Av?*

How many would have been enough
to make us question,
where was the redemption?

How many would have been enough
to leave our collective throat hoarse,
shrieking grief?

Did it have to be six million,
hunted and tortured and slaughtered in ways
that render inhumane mundane,
surpassing even our cultivated modern ability
to comprehend and describe?

How many, then?
What if a seep, not a deluge?
What if almost none?

Resonating Remembrance

Mourning Rituals

Decades of years have passed
since our people learned of the full extent,
watched as questionable, dubious, dismissible rumors
solidified into the unavoidably final catastrophe.

So many deaths.
If we honor their memory by mourning them as parents,
if we substitute a year for each day of the eleven month's grieving,
will our traditional rituals be adequate, not fail?

So many deaths.
The seven years of intense mourning, Shiva,
were interrupted by Israel's difficult birth after three,
suspended indefinitely by its embattled childhood.
Tradition gives precedence to *pikuach nefesh*,
to saving lives.

So many deaths.
Shloshim, now thirty years, not thirty days,
has whizzed past, moved too fast.
We have not begun to finish our laments.

So many deaths.
Counting all those Jews remaining,
half would be needed to recite Kaddish, morning and night,
for the eleven months become 330 years.

So many deaths.
Centuries will go by before we can name
their souls to rest in our children.

Holocaust Responsibilities

How many of them can fit in bed with us,
to share in our happiness, our precious security,
as we make love?
How many can we, braiding together in the act of life,
carry on our bodies?

Six million.
That's too many for our bed,
although I do manage to carry them around in my heart,
to reserve a corner dedicated to them in my head.

It's worse when I let the number dissolve into
individual people, individual faces.
I look at my son and daughter.
I imagine them being corrugated with me in a transport boxcar
and then, after who knows how long
without food, water, toilets,
our joy at being in the free, open air
shredded by the selection.

I read that sometimes mothers got a choice:
be gassed with the kids, or let the kids be gassed alone.
Bogus choice.
Mother eventually got gassed too.
Later, after she had been squeezed of her work juice,
the mother too would be gassed alone.

I look in the mirror and realize
women of my age did not survive.
They were not well represented among the
lebn-geblibene.

How passive the Yiddish.
Geblibene in lebn.
Stayed in life.
Remained in life.

How bewildering that label would have felt
to the minority *lebn-geblibene* shunted off toward barracks
when the majority was moving the other way,
toward death.

Death,
the popular "in" thing.
Surviving,
behind-in-life-staying,
the splinter group "out."

I snarf up their stories,
never fast enough, limited by my two input device eyes.
How many *lebn-geblibene* were there?
Not all of them wrote their stories down.

The *lebn-geblibene* don't need space allocation in our bed,
on our bodies.
They were remaindered to finish their own lives,
have daughters and sons by themselves.

If I feel responsible for six million,
I who was born after it was all over,
how much more must they stagger,
they who knew them, in person,
they who loved them, in person,
who watched them shrink, sink, subside, succumb, cease,
in person.

Never mind us, we of the first generation—
how did they, the *lebn-geblibene,*
manage to make love, act life, at all?

What Happened to the Children?

Our young daughter, seven, brimming with glee,
finally found the question:
"In the concentration camps,
what happened to the children?"

All the times we'd talked of then,
she, our artistic font, listened carefully
to the deadlife our words were painting.
Puzzled, she listened without ever facing up to
"What would have happened to me?"

"The children too," we answered
as we'd answered for ourselves.
"For them, first, too, the gas."
We left out the ovens and the ash.

"I can hold my breath forever,
or at least a day or two.
They wouldn't get me. Better not try."
She pulled herself back inside,
away from the brutal twist of knowing,
from the sucking void of knowing.

Her child weakness—
drawing lode for caring, hugs, protection—
would have in that bare, barbed yard
guaranteed immediate selection.
By being herself, as she is today,
she too would surely no longer be.

Embracing the Others

She cuddles in, loving.
She's warm, soft, and gorgeous,
vibrantly breathing, so fine.

"Concentrate on me, Mommy,"
her seven-year-old mouth,
demanding attention, lightly whines.

Better I shouldn't.
Better mindless enjoy her.
The visiting echoes too quickly resound.

The others, the others,
how many the others,
their mothers denied what I have?

The others, the others surround us,
their trace in our embrace
intertwined.

Survironies

Family History

WHEN AS A child I found out that both sides of my family had left Russia and emigrated to North America in 1913, just shy of the outbreak of the First World War, I was thrilled by the close call. Even if my parents had survived the upheavals of that war and the Russian Revolution that followed, I knew they probably would have perished when the Nazis stormed through.

It is certainly this sense of being at least a little charmed by fate, which my mother's writings also express, that tinges the poems in this section. The subject matter for the first two poems was distilled directly from those writings, some of which I have posted online at http://skyscribed.com/category/others/frances-c-sky/. The incident described in the first poem, "Scrambled Eggs Thicken the Plot," occurred when my mother, named Fruma as a child, was perhaps five or six and still living in the shtetl. In the second poem, "Inheritance Tricks," I have adopted my mother as the narrator who is telling the story of her family's emigration to me, her intently listening daughter.

Scrambled Eggs Thicken the Plot

Belka,
my mother's bit-older cousin,
stole the bird's egg
my child mother had finally found,
the egg Bubbie Anna said
would make her thin tresses
look full and round.

Belka,
pretending just to consider,
snatched the egg
and ran straight home.
Uneven race,
her shoe-shod feet
beat my mother's bare ones,
neat.

Belka
hid behind the door
my mother hit
with frantic fists
while rivulets of despair,
thicker even than her cousin's hair,
streamed down.

Belka
smirked into her mother's skirt
while auntie's whisking words of truth
shooed my mother off:
"Fruma, for goodness sake,
on your limp mop, what difference would
one egg make?"

Belka,
thirty-some years later,
perished,
thick locks presumably intact.
My mother,
her head still sparsely covered,
flourished,
knowing Tante Manya would have given
a thousand golden eggs
to have Belka usurp her
once more.

Inheritance Tricks

Once upon a time, my daughter,
you had a great-grandfather, a horse trader, rich,
with orchards, deep, behind his winged house
and drawers of coins within.

No help to us, waiting for the summons
from your grandfather, my father, the disinherited second son,
to come join him in America.
Six, then five when my oldest brother left too,
in one thatched roof room,
we were spurned, scratching, gasping, poor
between rescuing subsistence letters.

One letter, though, mysteriously, we never received,
the one that announced surrender.
We were to stay.
Father would, as Mother urged,
return and stake a claim to his rightful share
of Grandfather's plentiful tender.

Missing our cue,
we left for Glasgow, the Atlantic, Ellis Island,
and a home in New Britain, Connecticut.

I still imagine my uncle celebrating
his uncontested fortune, no trifle,
behind our receding backs.
Not for long, we later heard;
Bolshevik rifles stopped short his victory revels.
Uncle was shot, Great-grandfather too, against a wall.
All the rest—who knows how—must have fallen prey
to the Nazi devils.

And so, my darling, my dear, my daughter,
here on the safe side of the ocean,
you and me, all my father's family,
we were the ones who ultimately inherited
your great-grandfather's most precious legacy:
life.

Living on Borrowed Time

When will I have to resign
this borrowed time on which I live,
and who will the bailiff be?

Separately but simultaneously,
both my feeder branches left Russia,
unaware, but just in time,
before the Great War I would have trapped them,
in the shtetl pen, in the city cage,
kept them and their issue there,
to save them up like heedless, hapless geese
for the Great War II,
the thorough one.

Accidents of history, quirks of fate,
rescued me from
the wall,
the open pit,
the gas chamber.
It would not have been me but me anyhow
who perished.

Today, too,
accidents of history, quirks of fate,
rescue me.
In the synagogues, the Jewish-owned stores,
the kosher restaurants, the buses, the streets,
by bomb, gun, or knife,
it is not me but me anyhow
who perishes.

If it is ever really me,
the Jew who is slaughtered only for being a Jew,
no surprise at the reckoning.

Leaving in Time

The dense shadows looming, the painted warnings dripping,
would we have left there in time?

The edicts' clear clues: "Get out, you damned, you Jews."
Would we have heeded in time?

Would we have packed up quickly, not at our leisure,
moving our household in time?

Would we have sought out an adequate refuge—
not Holland or France but the New World—in time?

Who has the perfect perspective?
Who has the unfailing wisdom to react correctly, in time?

We still face the problem throughout daily living—
ours, less lethal now, than theirs, more fatal then.

It's chance, micro-written,
this divining the best route for surviving, in time.

Modern Response

Cherished Routine

We make the same motions each month—
same destined payments, same needed actions—
repetitive, dull, and boring too. Goo.
Even new variations, welcome distractions,
founder, encumbered by entangling strings.

Not the life we imagined.
The tradeoffs dismember our glowing intentions,
obscure our bright dreams with opaque residue.

How did we get here?
How did we end up materiel sentries,
distressed about objects, logistics, and time?
How did we get here?
We thought we were tending our ripening future
not our subtle decline.

We posture like doomed ones,
bemoan our fracturing, illusive fate,
until we remember, regain sober insight.

Viewed from our history,
the daily always was and always will be
a sumptuous respite.

Transmuting Evil

Why is egregious, execrable evil abundant,
inexorably fecund still?

Everyday evil's vile persistence I almost understand,
when regrettable but inevitable human differences
careen into full-fledged hostilities and wars.

But infernal evil in its ever-changing guises?
What powers the energy transforming human creativity
into hideous, premeditated insanity?

Why can so many living today
storm across the gulf that separates
ensuring my group's survival from
committing your group's genocide?

Weren't the blasts from the rockets, the nuclear bombs,
hot enough to extirpate that capability from our human genome?

Didn't this last century's cleaving of multimillions of life lines
cut deep enough to scar the border indelibly
so that all, all, all, all, all,
even those who proclaim they love dying
more than others love living,
eschew crossing the boundary
with the undeniable, visceral abhorrence
of violating a primal taboo?

Enough naive questions from my pen.
Lamarckian theory trounced again.

Israel, Anytime

They stone us.
They stab us.
They shoot us.
They bomb us.

Alarmed, angry, anguished,
determined to stay,
we swat them, we smash them.
They won't go away.

We feel for them.
We remember how being trapped is,
cornered in a powerless hell,
so desperate that risking death's knell equals release.

Until we encounter the persistent fanatics,
pursuing fallacious eternal salvation,
who wreak destruction on innocent others
and not solely on themselves.

Until we remember empathy's dangers.
What possible peaceful accommodation might pertain
to those who want our all?

When they say they want to annihilate us,
dump Israel into the unparted sea,
we Jews everywhere must take them dead serious.

We must forsake feckless, universalist cocoons
as if they will unravel into the true path to peace
instead of express lanes straight to our end.

We must defend.
Never Again.

Toy Guns

What is it we think we're achieving,
we members of the first generation,
when we ape them, the so morally upright,
in denying our children toy guns?

When we successfully stop the kids
from using even their fingers to pretend,
how can we so smugly congratulate ourselves
as if we'd finally discovered the secret
to eliminating fighting and wars instead of
to ensuring our own demise?

As others mouth,
with trite platitudes dressed up as creeds,
the unquestioned evils of guns,
how can we buy into their babbling,
sagely agree, approvingly acquiesce?

As Jews,
we should never forget what we know from experience.
For our own really dependable, long-term security,
having our own guns to defend ourselves
is essential.

We must understand our reality.
Denying our children toy guns reflects
our own dangerous fuzziness about
what our history has taught us we need to survive
when our persistent enemies threaten,
not our virtue as modern parents.

Sentencing God

A. *The Charge*
So, where
Praised Be God,
Baruch Adonai,
where were
You,
Attah?

Was it no business of Yours
when six million of the stiffest-necked, the most stubborn,
Your people,
got it in the neck?

I would need
the muscle ratio of grasshopper legs
to leap my leaps of faith
far enough away to avoid that question.
I would have to leap clear into the oblivion of lobotomy,
disqualifying me as a suitable partner,
as an in-Your-Image partner,
for You.

Praised Be Our God,
Baruch Eloheinu,
You,
Attah,
where the hell were You
from 1933 to 1945?

You,
You and Your Whereabouts,
You and Your Intentions,
You and Your Actions
are on trial
for what You did,
for what You did not do.

B. My Authority
By what authority can the finite challenge the Infinite?
By what authority can the finite not challenge the Infinite
after what happened?

What would it look like
for the finite to challenge the Infinite?
Could it look like this poem?
Is this the right forum for calling You to task,
condemning Your Turpitude, exposing Your Transgression
against all the Moral Laws of Your Universe?

Right forum or not,
it's what I've got.
It's what I'm using.

C. The Theological Defense
Stuck in our finite world, we cannot know
Your Infinity,
Your Plans for us,
Plans in which—theologian Fackenheim said—
still we must believe.

Without our mutual choosing of
THE SPECIAL RELATIONSHIP
between us—
You and Jews—
what explanation is there for whatever glues Jews,
surviving-for-so-many-years Jews,
together with each other?

Without Your Existence,
what meaning?

D. My Verdict
With Your Existence,
what meaning?

You have sinned grievously.
An eternity of Yom Kippurs
would not give You enough time
to repent, atone, become at-one again.

You are not worthy of our love.
You are not worthy of our worship.
You are not worthy of our attention.
You are not worthy of our consideration
for what You did,
for what You did not do.

For what You did,
for what You did not do,
I don't care about Your Plans for history.
I don't care about Your Plans for Jews.
I don't care about Your Plans for me.

For what You did,
for what You did not do,
I condemn You to be ignored
even as I continue to be a Jew.

For what You did,
for what You did not do
I BREAK OUR COVENANT.

I'm guessing even those at Sinai
would support my action.

Given your behavior,
what you did
what you did not do,
they would most certainly applaud my intention
to be a Jew
without you.

Afterword: Germany
in October 1993

W E BEGAN OUR visit to Germany in 1993 by first meeting our friends in Weimar, in the former East Germany, before continuing on to Berlin, our ultimate destination. When we returned home, I wrote an afterword to the original *First Generation Singular* poems.

Visiting Germany while Visiting Germany
This trip to Germany initially left me feeling uneasy, ambiguous. I enjoy our friends, speaking German, but visiting Germany is an experience I somehow still question: Why vacation here? Am I not betraying the memory of the six million just by being here?

Take the Martin-Gropius-Bau in Berlin, which I later found out was formerly SS headquarters. How could I go to enjoy art in the building that once housed those directing my people's persecution? How could I obliviously view its exhibits from within a context of normalcy? I am ashamed I did not know. Naiveté is no excuse. Or take Buchenwald, just outside Weimar. How could we have *visited* it? Quietly observing, politely behaving ourselves doesn't suffice. But that is what we did.

After talking over my reaction to this most recent trip with my family, I have developed another, somewhat different perspective. Being in the former East Germany, not the former West Germany, is what ripped open my scabs.

We had travelled to the former East once before as a family, very purposefully, in October 1991, so the children would have a chance to see what the Communists had wrought before the reunified Germany began to reconstruct and renovate the degradation into disappearance. As a result of missing the same train twice in Prague—a feat more humorous in the retelling than in the enduring—we saw a piece of the former East Germany not on our original route. Instead of going directly from Prague to Berlin, we ended up spending some four or five hours in the Dresden train station. There we had one of the adventures that we have since, in a wry phrase coined by our son, come to label a "how nice it is to be able to visit Germany while visiting Germany" experience.

While I was off somewhere, probably in the ladies' room, my husband and the kids saw a group of three or four drunken German guys in their late teens or early twenties harassing a man whom we thought was probably a *Gastarbeiter*, a foreign worker temporarily living in Germany. They threw drink cans at him and then, getting bolder, grabbed him by the collar, trying to drag him down. He kept shrugging them off and moving forward until they lost interest.

Of course my husband immediately went to the door of the *Polizeiabteilung* (the police department) in the train station. After banging on the door, he was able to tell someone what was happening. The reaction? "*Wir kommen gleich.*" (We're coming right away.) Anyone who has heard that expression, for example, from the mouth of a German waiter, knows it really means, "In my own good time."

And then there was our very own "visiting Germany while visiting Germany" experience in Weimar. Our first night there, before any of our friends had arrived, we went to the *Zwiebelmarkt*, the open-air collection of food booths and festivities celebrating the onion harvest. After eating a delicious meal of many incompatible delectables purchased from various vendors, we walked around, exploring the shops along Schiller Street, a pedestrian mall. We stopped to look in the window of an antique bookstore, my husband and daughter slightly off to the side. From certain angles, given that our son was already taller than me, I was probably not visible.

Our son, his curly dark-brown hair in its customary Revolutionary War queue, was wearing one of his finer jackets that evening, a brown-leather item he had overpaid a quarter for at a thrift shop in northern Wisconsin. His hair and jacket, not to mention his rather distinctively non-Aryan (Italian? Turkish? Greek? Jewish?) features, apparently signaled "foreigner who needs some roughing up" to three, perhaps drunken, German youths. Out of the corner of my eye, I saw them select him. They came over. To begin the encounter, they bumped into him, revealing me and—when our eyes went immediately to my husband and daughter—making it clear that we were together. A family!

None of us remember exactly what happened then. One of the blond-crewcut guys came up to my husband and asked him, belligerently, "*Was hast du gesagt?*" (What did you [familiar] say?) "*Ich habe nichts gesagt,*" (I didn't say anything.) answered my husband. Feeling emboldened, I glared at the young toughs. After all, we were in the midst of a crowded shopping street, not in a deserted train station, and people would certainly come to our aid if we were really attacked.

Shrugging and posturing appropriately, our son's assailants backed off. Perhaps they realized that we were American and therefore not the right kind of foreigner. Or perhaps it just wouldn't be as much fun attacking a whole family. Shaken, we huddled together to try to make sense out of what had happened.

Was it coincidence that both times we were in the former East, we were involved in the kinds of incidents that recall the Nazi era? Who knows? In a whole month by himself in the former West Germany, our son had had no similar encounters. In over two years in the former West Germany, living in Frankfurt and traveling extensively throughout the country, neither had we.

If I had been more attentive to the implications of both incidents, less willing to ascribe the glow from our own positive experiences equally to both parts of the unified country, perhaps I would have been better prepared for what we found at Buchenwald, one of the first concentration camps on German soil, located on Etter Mountain, near Goethe's Weimar.

Our Buchenwald

Dedicated to the memory of Heinz Warschauer

Driving around Weimar,
looking for the road to our reunion hotel,
Zum Alten Gutshof,
inadvertently we found the road to our reunion charnel,
nach Buchenwald.

"Is this our Buchenwald?"
I mused as, oddly drawn, we turned up to the left, the wrong way,
to follow the pointed yellow route sign.
More than once before,
I had mistakenly heard a Holocaust echo
in an innocent German town's name.
Yet how many Buchenwalds could there be?

There to pay homage where German culture flourished,
we moved "pay respects where German culture defecated"
to the top of our itinerary.

Up to the left the next day, this time purposely.
Up the straight road,
past vast forest tracts,
past abandoned army camps faced by slabs of concrete wall,
forbidden by stands of warning signs saying,
>   Former military area
>   *Lebensgefahr*
>   Danger to life.

Up the straight road
that had led straight to Lebensgefahr
for the reluctantly marching feet
whose muffled tramps were shaken loose by our tires
in a fast-forward hum.

Straight up the road, our bodies were transported
quickly, effortlessly, in our Spanish Volkswagen SEAT,
to the *Mahndenkmal*, the memorial that gives warning:
Buchenwald.

Tense with anticipation—
What would we find? Would it be too rending?—
we parked and surveyed the schematic map,
a convenient overview of the whole camp at one glance.

Bookstore first.
Verbal analysis distancing emotional paralysis.
That we could handle.

Down the path,
through the maroon main gate, in such fine shape.
Past the *Kommandant*'s quarters,
windows curtained in light puke-green with white lace.
Were they original?

Our silent questions
buffered our bewildered steps forward toward the past:
Zachor, Remember!

Anguish that it had been—that it existed still—
contended with gratitude that we could bear witness
as Disneyland-like lenses deflected our stares
from confronting our Buchenwald.

Purposeless ambiguity. Needless anguish.
I was mistaken once again.
This Buchenwald was not ours.

Ploughing through dense German institutional prose
adorning all—
    the rough, slotted cells,
    the neatly rubbled fields,
    the solemnly engraved black stone slabs,
    the artful museum displays—
we began to realize, with rancor and relief,
the irony of ironies:
according to the East German Communists,
this small remnant of our suffering places,
in final Nazi victory,
was totally *judenrein,* free of Jews!

Not Jews but Social Democrats, Communists, Soviet soldiers,
anti-fascists all,
found here not only slaughter, but a more subtle fate,
Vernichtung durch Arbeit,
extermination through labor.

This Buchenwald, eternally ours,
its history eradicated through contortions of
Ersatz-Nazi Communist officially reconstructed memory,
had become temporally theirs.

How much more a sign warning
Lebensgefahr,
can a memorial be?

Acknowledgments

"THIS IS NOT cheery reading," I said to those whom I asked if they would be willing to review the first draft of *First Generation Singular: Reactions to Living in Post-Holocaust Germany* and give me their reactions and comments. Nonetheless, most agreed to take on the task. My deepest thanks and gratitude go to everyone in that group of about a dozen readers for their time, careful attention, and encouragement that wider distribution for this collection of poems and prose would be worth pursuing.

Of the initial group of readers I want to mention three people by name: Joan Eisenberg, herself a poet, gifted me with comments from her close reading that probed softs spots and highlighted strengths; Annalee Letchinger, in addition to her positive comments, pointed out several crucial points where clarity failed; Douglas Hoffman, my husband, by dragging me off to West Germany in 1970 and making it possible for me to return in 1976, sowed the seeds for all that ultimately grew into *The Sky Family Festschrift*. In his careful review of the various incarnations of this collection, Doug made numerous cogent and extremely helpful comments as well as serving as my on call sounding board.

Finally, I want to thank those who worked on this book with me. Artist and author, Susan Bruck, took on and met the challenge of creating a cover that reflects the contents. Then there are the folk at CreateSpace: my publishing consultant, Jenny Legun Chandler, and the semi-anonymous members of my very responsive team, known to me by their first names only. Without them all, I am quite certain *First Generation Singular: Reactions to Living in Post-Holocaust Germany* would have remained just another document file on my computer's hard drive.

Es geht ohne sagen (it goes without saying) or, Doug tells me, more formally, *Es ist selbstverständlich* (of course), in the end I bear sole responsibility for everything that appears here.

About the Author

S HIRLEE SKY HOFFMAN is a retired marketing consultant and group facilitator. Born in Canada, she received her bachelor's degree in history from York University in Toronto and her master's degrees in history and in education from Harvard University. She and her family lived twice in West Germany in the 1970s.

Hoffman has written all her life. Her poems and short stories have been published in numerous books and periodicals and, more recently, on her website at www.skyscribed.com.

Hoffman lives with her husband in Chicago. When she isn't writing, she volunteers at the University of Chicago's Oriental Institute where she learns about the ancient Near East and delights in sharing her ever-growing knowledge with visitors of all ages.

Glossary

Arbetering	Workmen's Circle Association. (Yiddish)
Attah	You. (Hebrew)
Baruch Adonai	Praised be God. (Hebrew)
Baruch Eloheinu	Praised be our God. (Hebrew)
Bubbie	Grandmother. (Yiddish)
Channukah	An eight-day festival celebrated by lighting an additional candle each night. (Hebrew)
Das wäre es, danke.	That would be it (all I need), thank you. (German)
Du	You (second person singular, familiar). (German)
Eaton's	T. Eaton Co. Limited was a Canadian department store that went bankrupt in 1999.
Festschrift	A collection of writings that colleagues publish in honor of a scholar during his or her lifetime. (German and English)
Frau	Mrs. (German)

Gastarbeiter	A "guest worker," i.e., a foreigner who had permission to live and work temporarily in Germany. (German)
Geblibene in lebn	Stayed or remained in life. (Yiddish)
Guten Tag	Good day; hello. (German)
Gutskeit	The good one, of a person, affectionately. (Yiddish)
Havdalah	The ritual in Judaism marking the end of the Sabbath at sundown on Saturday; includes lighting a braided candle. (Hebrew)
Herr	Mr. (German)
Holocaust	"The systematic, bureaucratic, state-sponsored persecution and murder of six million Jews by the Nazi regime and its collaborators." http://www.ushmm.org
Hundert Gramm von dem, bitte.	A hundred grams of that, please. (German)
Ich habe nichts gesagt.	I didn't say anything. (German)
In den Laden	Into the store. (German)
JCC	Jewish Community Center.
Ja, Ja, das reicht.	Yes, yes, that's enough. (German)
Judenfrei	Free of Jews. (German)
Judenrein	Cleansed of Jews. (German)

Kaddish	Mourner's Kaddish, a prayer said for eleven months by Jews mourning a parent's death. (Aramaic)
Kommandant	Commander. (German)
Kvelling	To be extremely proud. (English from Yiddish)
Lamarckian	Jean-Baptiste Lamarck proposed a theory of inheritance of acquired characteristics.
Lebensgefahr	Danger to life. (German)
Lebn-geblibene	Those who stayed or remained in life. (Yiddish)
Mahndenkmal	Memorial thavt gives warning. (German)
Malthus	Thomas Robert Malthus wrote about pressures checking population growth.
Nach Buchenwald	Toward Buchenwald. (German)
Pale of Settlement	A western region of imperial Russia, established in 1791, in which Jews were allowed to live.
Pesach	Passover. A festival celebrating the deliverance of the Jewish people from slavery in Egypt through the Exodus. (Hebrew)
Pikuach nefesh	Saving a life; the principle in Judaism that the preservation of human life overrides virtually any other religious consideration. (Hebrew)

Polizeiabteilung	The police station. (German)
Rein	Pure, clean. (German)
SS	Initials for the Nazi Party's *Schutzstaffel* or "Protective Squadron." (German)
Schande	A disgrace. (Yiddish)
Shabbat	The Jewish Sabbath. (Hebrew)
Shiva	In Judaism, the week-long mourning period of staying at home ("sitting Shiva"), beginning after the funeral. (Hebrew)
Shloshim	In Judaism, the first thirty days of mourning after the funeral. (Hebrew)
Sie	You (second person singular, formal); also third person plural, "they." (German)
Tante	Aunt. (Yiddish)
Tisha B'Av	Ninth day of the Jewish calendar month of Av; annual fast day commemorating disasters in Jewish history. (Hebrew)
Treasured People	Treasured people or nation (*am segulah*) is a phrase that appears in Torah, the Five Books of Moses. (Hebrew)
Unter anderem	Among other things. (German)
Vernichtung durch Arbeit	Extermination through labor. (German)

Volkswagen	People's Car. (German)
Was hast du gesagt?	What did you (familiar) say? (German)
White steak	In Israel, a euphemism for pork.
Wir kommen gleich.	We're coming right away. (German)
Yahrtzeit	Year time. In Judaism, the anniversary of a death, marked by lighting a memorial candle. (Yiddish from German)
Yom HaShoah	Holocaust Remembrance Day; *shoah* means "catastrophe." (Hebrew)
Yom Kippur	The Day of Atonement, the holiest day in the Jewish year. (Hebrew)
Zachor	Remember. (Hebrew)
Zaide	Grandfather. (Yiddish)
Zum Alten Gutshof	Name of a Weimar hotel, "The Good Old Grange." (German)
Zwiebelmarkt	Onion market. An open-air celebration of the onion harvest. (German)